T0353804

Angel Whispers of Guidance and Inspiration

Carol Mulqueeney

Print information available on the last page

Rev. date: 08/25/2015

To order additional copies of this book, contact:
Xlibris
1-888-795-4274
www.Xlibris.com
Orders@Xlibris.com

Contents

STRENGTH, PROTECTION, TRUTH

Archangel Michael

© carol byrne

Archangel Michael being chosen by you is a reassurance to you that you are safe and protected. If this page was picked in answer to a question, it is telling you that you can call on Michael to bring the truth into a situation, because with truth comes strength.

Archangel Michael is a protector and a defender, and you can call on him in times of crisis. He will help you release any emotions or limiting behaviour that may be preventing you from moving on in your life.

Call on Michael to support you whenever you feel insecure or afraid. He will always be there to surround you with his powerful blue healing energy.

HEALING, WHOLENESS

Archangel Raphael

© carol byrne

Archangel Raphael is the Angel of healing and healers. Choosing this page is a sign that Raphael is here to help you with a situation that needs to be healed. This could be personal health, or perhaps something is happening in your life right now, that needs Raphael's healing energy to help resolve an issue for the highest good of all concerned.

You can call on Raphael whenever you need healing for yourself or for someone else, ask him to share his beautiful green healing energy, for the good of all who need healing in their lives at this time.

GUIDANCE, INSPIRATION

Archangel Gabriel

© carol byrne

Archangel Gabriel is the Angel of Guidance. When you are unsure of which direction to take in life, call on Archangel Gabriel to help you find the way forward. Gabriel will open your mind to other options and inspire you by giving you ideas, and presenting you with opportunities that might otherwise be overlooked.

If you chose this page in a spread with other pages, pay particular attention to the words and guidance around it, as they may be a message from Archangel Gabriel.

TRANSFORMATION, WISDOM, LIGHT

Archangel Uriel

© carol byr

Archangel Uriel is the Angel of Transformation; he can help you with any situation. Uriel encourages you to talk to him about what in your life needs changing. He asks you to look at all the relationships in your life, be it family, work colleagues or friends.

If there is negativity surrounding any area of your life, call on Archangel Uriel to use his red and amber energy to transmute any negativity into positive energies of healing.

He tells you that in times of crisis he will help you find peace amidst the chaos, as he brings wisdom and light to you to help weather the storm.

SPIRITUALITY, FORGIVENESS

Archangel Zadkiel

© carol byrne

Archangel Zadkiel is the Angel of Spirituality; he will help you with your spiritual development. He will also help you with any issues of forgiveness you may have.

Forgiveness is a great healer, by holding on to a limiting emotion you are allowing negative energies to build up, which in turn can cause illness and stress, which in turn again, can affect your relationships with others.

Zadkiel will help you now to transmute any dense, negative energies into positive healing energies.

JOY, ILLUMINATION

Archangel Jophiel

© carol byrne

Archangel Jophiel appears to you today, to help you find your inner light. Sometimes in life, it is easy to forget you are a child of joy and light. Everyday living takes over, and it feels as if the sunshine has gone from your heart. Jophiel will help you bring the light back into your life, he encourages you to play and have fun, to learn to laugh again.

The more you look for things that make you smile, the more joy you allow back in. So whenever you feel sad or under the weather, call on Jophiel to send light and joy into your life.

COMPASSION, UNCONDITIONAL LOVE

Archangel Chamuel

© carol byrne

Archangel Chamuel is the Angel of peaceful relationships. By being drawn to this page today, you are being guided to work on your relationships.

Ask Archangel Chamuel to help you resolve any conflicts in your life, and to shine his beautiful pink ray on you, to heal and nurture.

Chamuel's pink healing ray will surround you with unconditional love, and will help you to give and receive love, unconditionally and free from self interest.

THE BOOK OF LIFE

Archangel Metatron comes to you today to help you find your way in life. Metatron is witness to all the good you do in life and will help you reach your full potential.

He will help you find balance and fulfillment, and give you inspiring ideas, to encourage you to follow the path that is right for you.

Pay extra attention to any new ideas or flashes of inspiration that come your way.

LOVE IS THE BEAUTY OF THE SOUL

When we give or receive love, unconditionally and with no preconceived motives, our soul shines brighter.

To be able to love and receive love unconditionally brings the beauty of our soul to the surface.

SPIRITUAL GROWTH

spiritual

growth

© carol byrne

You are on the path of spiritual growth. You are becoming aware of many different spiritual and holistic practices and ways of being.

Maybe treat yourself to a therapy, or sit and meditate, to experience the stillness that encourages spiritual growth.

EVERYTHING HAPPENS IN DIVINE ORDER AND FOR THE HIGHEST GOOD

everything happens
in divine order
and for the
highest good

© carol byrne

Have you been waiting for a desired outcome, feeling that things were never going to work out for you?

These words are a message that sometimes you have to wait a bit longer.

It will happen... maybe not when you want... or how you want, but when the time is right and for the good of all concerned.

So be patient and trust that it will work out for the best

THE PAST IS BEHIND YOU

the past
is behind
you

© carol byrne

This picture shows you that you have to take back your power and leave your past exactly where it is …'in the past'.

By carrying the shadow of your past with you throughout your whole life, you are creating a barrier, preventing new hope and new experiences from entering your life.

So take back your power now and leave your past in the past.

LET YOUR TRUE SELF EMERGE

let your
    true self
        emerge

© carol byrne

Are you being true to yourself? Or are you so used to being who others expect you to be?

When you live in a way... or feel in a way that is not truly you... you can never be truly happy.

Let your true self emerge now, and see how your happiness evolves to another level.

Feel the beauty of your true self shine through.

NURTURE YOUR INNER CHILD

nurture

your

inner child

© carol byrne

It is very important to remember that your own emotions also need tending to at times. Be gentle with yourself and love yourself completely.

Send love to the 'younger you', your childhood self.

If there are any fears or insecurities that you may have carried from your childhood into your adult life, call on Archangel Chamuel to help you.

Chamuel is the Angel of compassion and unconditional love, and will help you with your emotions. He will help you nurture your inner child and bring peace to your life.

RELEASE YOUR FEARS

release

your

fears.

© carol byrne

By holding on to your fears you are creating a reality of negativity,
leaving no room for joy or positivity to enter your life.

Let go of your fears by sitting quietly, breathing deeply and on the outbreath,
visualise your fears leaving your body and mind. See, feel or sense as they are blown
towards the clouds and carried away from you... now breathe in love and joy.

You can also call on Archangel Michael to help you by
surrounding you with his powerful blue energy.

LET GO AND LET GOD

let go
and
let God.

© carol byrne

This page indicates that you have asked for help with a particular issue.
You need to trust that God has heard your prayer. Leave it in Gods hands
now and stop trying to fix it with ways that are your own.

By not letting go you are interfering with Gods plans to bring this issue to a satisfactory conclusion.

FEATHERS APPEAR WHEN ANGELS ARE NEAR

feathers
appear
when angels
are near.

© carol byrne

Have you ever noticed a feather float gently to the floor, or have you perhaps found a feather in a place you would never expect?

The Angels send feathers to bring your awareness to the fact that they are around you.

Sometimes to let you know that your prayers have been heard, at other times to remind you that you are not alone.

By picking this page today the Angels are trying to attract your attention.

MEDITATE FOR INNER PEACE

meditate for inner peace

© carol byrne

You have been drawn to this page because you need to spend some time away from the hustle and bustle of life. Your thoughts are working overtime right now.

Find a way to meditate, so you can quiet your mind and experience the deep inner peace that comes with meditation.

LET YOUR LIGHT SHINE

let your
light
shine.

© carol byrne

You have so much to offer the world. Come out of the shadow
of other people and let your light shine through.

It is time to light up your life and shine, so that both you and those around
you can benefit from the true, authentic light energy that is you.

THERE IS ALWAYS A WAY

there is

always

a way.

© Carol byrne

At times you feel stuck or trapped, as you try to find a resolution to a problem. You may feel there is no way out of a situation... 'there is always a way'...

You need to step back and look at this matter objectively.

The page that follows this one in a reading may have more information to help you.

SIGNS OF LOVE FROM HEAVEN ABOVE

signs of love
        from heaven
                above

© carol byrne

The Angels are letting you know you are loved. They send signs to reassure you that you are a precious child of God. They surround you with the energy of love at times when you need it most.

OPEN YOUR HEART TO MIRACLES

This photograph shows you that by being open to miracles coming into your life, you create an energy that attracts good and positive things to you.

So believe... and accept that miracles 'do' happen... and 'can' happen for you.

FORGIVE YOURSELF AND OTHERS

forgive
yourself
and others

© carol byrne

You are being asked to forgive yourself for any part you may have played by actions, thoughts or deeds, against another.

In turn you are asked to forgive others who may, intentionally or otherwise, have caused you hurt in any way.

By offering up this forgiveness, you are opening your heart to receiving love and blessings that may have been blocked before

EMBRACE HARMONY IN YOUR LIFE

embrace harmony
in your life

© carol byrne

You have peace and harmony in your life right now. Embrace this feeling and enjoy the effect it has on you and everyone you come in contact with.

When you feel good... You attract good.

SAY YES TO BLESSINGS THAT ARE ON THE WAY

You are about to receive blessings of love and abundance.

Accept these blessings graciously and with gratitude.

PEACE AND TRANQUILITY

peace
and
tranquillity

© carol byrne

Spend some time in a place that brings calm to your mind. A place of beauty and serenity.

By spending time in a peaceful and tranquil environment, you are healing
your emotions and your ability to deal with everyday life.

THIS TOO WILL PASS

this too

will

pass.

© carol byrne

When everything seems stormy and troubles are mounting up around you, when you are consumed with guilt, sadness, fear or anger, just remember these words... 'this too will pass'.

By doing this you are not accepting it as a final or lasting time in your life, and as the words imply, it will pass, and your life will open up to new possibilities.

YOUR PRAYERS ARE BEING ANSWERED

your prayers
are being
answered.

© carol byrn

God and the Angels know you have been praying for a particular outcome.

They are letting you know that your prayers are being answered,
for the highest good of all concerned.

LOOK FORWARD TO NEW BEGINNINGS

look forward
to new
beginnings

© carol byrne

You may have changes going on in your life that are causing concern. Instead of focusing on the word ' change ' (which can be quite intimidating at times) look on it as a new beginning.

Look forward to the new in your life, and the excitement and possibilities a new beginning can bring.

HOPE AND EXPECTANCY

This page encourages you to have hope and a sense of excitement.

You can be inclined to get yourself stuck in a rut, feeling as if this is all there is.

By having hope and expectancy in your life, you are open to new ideas and ventures, which in turn bring the light and joy into your life.

CELEBRATE... GOOD NEWS IS ON THE WAY

celebrate.
good news
is on the way

© carol blabe

You are put on notice to expect good news which is coming your way.

IN OUR DARKEST HOURS
WE ARE NEVER ALONE

in our
darkest hours
we are never
alone.

© carol byrne

When you are at your lowest, and sadness and grief have darkened your life, this message is sent to reassure you and tell you that even if you can't see it right now, God and the Angels are with you.

They will support you and give you the strength to carry on... You are never alone.

SPEAK YOUR TRUTH

You are being advised to always speak your truth. By doing so
you are creating an energy of strength and power.

By being your authentic self, instead of what someone else wants, you
attract good into your life, because you are being true to yourself.

LOOK DEEPER TO FIND CLARITY

You have to look past what appears to be the norm. If a situation has presented itself into your life and if you have any doubts or uneasiness about it, you need to look past the façade .

By looking deeper you will discover the truth.

Printed in the United States
By Bookmasters